soul detox

LYNNE THEMELARAS, M.A.

Soul Detox © 2024 by Lynne Themelaras.
All rights reserved.

Published by:
Resound International Ministries
Westerville, OH 43082
www.BillandLynne.com

All rights reserved.
This book contains materials protected by international and Federal Copyright Laws and Treaties. Any unauthorized reprint or use of this material is prohibited. No part of this book may be reproduced or transmitted in any form or by means, electronic or mechanical, including photocopying, recording, or by any information storage and retrieval system, without express written permission by the author.

Identifier:
ISBN: 9798861439954 (paperback)

dedication

I am deeply grateful to the Holy Spirit for guiding me towards personal healing, enabling me to write this book. I extend my heartfelt thanks to my husband, Bill Themelaras, for his unwavering support, encouragement, and the time he provided for my healing process. My beautiful children always lifted my spirits, making me feel like a rockstar with their words of encouragement. Lastly, I must mention my dear friend Monica Guidry, who remained my constant cheerleader, persistently urging me to publish my book even during moments of self-doubt.

contents

Acknowledgments	11
Foreword	13
Endorsements	17
Introduction	21

WEEK ONE

Day 1	27
Day 2	33
Day 3	36
Day 4	39
Day 5	42

WEEK TWO

Day 6	47
Day 7	51
Day 8	54
Day 9	57
Day 10	60

WEEK THREE

Day 11	65
Day 12	68
Day 13	70
Day 14	72
Day 15	74

WEEK FOUR

Day 16	79
Day 17	82
Day 18	85
Day 19	88
Day 20	90

WEEK FIVE

Day 21	95
Day 22	97
Day 23	100
Day 24	103
Day 25	105

WEEK SIX

Day 26	111
Day 27	115
Day 28	118
Day 29	121
Day 30	124

WEEK SEVEN

Day 31	131
Day 32	134
Day 33	137
Day 34	140
Day 35	143

WEEK EIGHT

Day 36	149
Day 37	151
Day 38	154
Day 39	157
Day 40	160
Bibliography	165
Ways to connect with the author	167

Soul Detox

A Path to Renewal and Restoration

acknowledgments

Edited by: Niah Themelaras
Formatted by: Renalta Nkansah
Book cover by: Cullen Themelaras

foreword

> "But solid food is for the mature, whose spiritual senses perceive heavenly matters. And they have been adequately trained by what they've experienced to emerge with understanding of the difference between what is truly excellent and what is evil and harmful."
> Hebrews 5:14 (TPT)

Brian Simmons's translation of this critical passage from the Book of Hebrews is a profound description of the journey and the life message of someone who has embraced the dealings of the Father that produce a picture of a true and empowering maturity. Often, I'll read a passage from the scriptures, and it will remind me of someone I have known over the years. This passage and the Apostle Paul's description of Timothy's "proven worth" in Philippians 2:22, NASB95 are kindred verses.

My wife, Barbara, and I have known Lynne Themelaras for over two decades. She and her husband, Apostle Bill Themelaras, serve as the senior leaders of Oasis City Church, an amazing community of believers, which they planted with Adam and Tara Stewart twelve years ago in Westerville, Ohio, a suburb of Columbus, Ohio. However, our journey with Lynne began when she and two young children joined her husband, who became a part of our ministry team at Covenant Church in the early 2000s. As Joseph's gifts "made room for him" in Pharaoh's court, Lynne's administrative skills and creative gifting quickly answered our church's need for a qualified leader of our daycare center. Eventually, she became the Children's Pastor for our growing ministry. Lynne was a valuable addition to our ministry team, as she demonstrated the administrative and creative attributes those two positions desperately needed.

One of my mentors once told me, "There are only two kinds of churches: the ones that are dealing with their problems and the ones that are not." In retrospect, Lynne had to deal with the problems of the dysfunctions of a growing and flourishing church that had problems, and by natural disposition, she was a problem solver. There were challenges on two fronts, at church and at home. Her oldest daughter, Niah, had received a challenging health diagnosis. Lynne became a fierce advocate for the dietary restrictions essential for her total recovery, which was incidentally phenomenal; Niah recently graduated from college with honors. At the same time, she was raising two other children: a son, Cullen, and Skylar, a foster daughter, who they adopted. The disciplines necessary to achieve these and other goals have contributed significantly to so much that is also structurally sound in Lynne's spiritual walk.

When Lynne and Bill moved to Westerville, Ohio, she carried the tools and disciplines forged in the furnace of relationships and perseverance. You don't readily recognize significant changes that are taking place in a person's life when you're close and personal in your daily relationships. However, when some distance occurs in time and space, you are often startled by the reality of what could appear to be phenomenal growth. This growth results from something Eugene Peterson calls *A Long Obedience In The Same Direction*. Lynne was no longer my Children's Church pastor; she was now a pastor in her own right, and it seemed like a metaphor for Aaron's rod that had blossomed and bore fruit overnight!

"So Jesus said to the Jews who had believed him, "If you abide in my word, you are truly my disciples, and you will ***know*** the truth, and the truth will set you free" John 8:31 - 32 (*ESV*). Lynne is manifesting the freedom that comes from abiding in His word. Her growth has come from ***doing*** what the word of God teaches. Correct teaching is called *orthodoxy*, and correct living is called *orthopraxy*. Jesus validated the right teaching of the Pharisees. However, He strictly warned His disciples against following their example in living. You can only come to know intimately the truth by regularly abiding in the word. The writer of Hebrews 5:14 (*ESV*) says, "But solid food is for the mature, for those who have their powers of discernment trained by constant practice to distinguish good from evil." This devotional is written by a practitioner trained through faithful and consistent practice. Pastor Lynne Themelaras is not a theorist; ask anyone she has counseled, advised, or encouraged at Oasis or Covenant. Much like the Apostle Paul, she is saying, "Follow me ***as*** I follow Christ." *Soul Detox* is a powerful spiritual application that will demonstrate, when followed, that **Truth Works!**

Bishop Joseph L. Garlington
President
Reconciliation! An International Network of Churches and Ministries

Endorsements

Are you looking for a personal change, even personal revival? Soul Detox can lead you into fresh God encounters and empowerment. Using an inspired structure, Soul Detox, incorporates scripture, journaling, reflection, and commitment to action as Lynne helps you navigate some of the greatest issues we as Christians face.

Lynne so beautifully guides you without being controlling. She encourages without trivializing the complexity of issues, and lays out Godly principles without being preachy or judgmental. This is a book for today. Following Lynne's detox program will bring you closer to God as well as closer to being God's best you.

Chester and Betsy Kylstra
Founders of Restoring the Foundations Ministries
Founders of Transforming Your Business / Ministry

Soul detox is a unique devotional written from the heart through experience to help bring readers into a greater degree of freedom and understanding of the importance of the health of our souls.

My dear friend Lynne has captured perfectly thecomparison between physical and soul health, highlighting the importance of detoxing our souls as well as our bodies so that we become more like Jesus.

This daily devotional is packed with juicy tips and advice that take readers on a beautiful journey of unpacking their past wounds and detoxing the soul as the Holy Spirit brings healing and deliverance to areas of our lives that need a touch from Him. I personally have been through seasons of detoxing and I highly recommend this daily devotional to help lead you into a lifestyle of freedom and transformation .

Chloe Glassborow
Co-Founder of I Believe Foundation
Conference Speaker & TBN Show host
Artist
@chloeglassborow

God created each of us *because* He has a Father's heart. He wanted sons and daughters to relate to. He loves each and every one of us with a love greater than we can even fathom. John, the beloved apostle, shares: "See what great love the Father has lavished on us, that we should be called children of God! And that is what we are!" (1 John 3:1).

The word for *love* in this verse is *agape,* and it refers to an abundance of love—a love feast. It captures the deepest aspect of God's nature—He *is* love. It is from this place of loving the Father and receiving His love for us that we are able to love ourselves and others. It is here that we are empowered to become and to walk in all that God has destined for us.

The prophet Isaiah tells us, "You will guard him and keep him in perfect and constant peace whose mind [both its inclination and its character] is stayed on You, because he commits himself to You, leans on You, and hopes confidently in You" (Isa. 26:3, amp). When we set our minds on Him, on the truth of His Word, and on the love and goodness of our Heavenly Father, our souls will be cleansed and healed and we will experience perfect peace. Not only that, but we will be strengthened to walk according to God's Word in our full identity as His sons and daughters.

As Lynne so beautifully states, "We can make choices to cultivate our inner selves with positive thoughts, emotional healing, and spiritual growth." Friends this devotional and message is life changing. Step into the journey of healing, wholeness and empowerment. Thank you Lynne for this life transforming message.

Rebecca Greenwood
Cofounder,
Christian Harvest International
Strategic Prayer Apostolic Network

Lynne Themelaras' new devotional book, "Soul Detox" is a journey to freedom through the transformational power of the

ENDORSEMENTS

Lord. Lynn's relational style of writing offers practical tools and wisdom to develop a lifestyle of health, healing and renewal.

John 10:10 reminds us that Jesus came to give us life and life abundantly and through the power of Scripture, healing prayer and the revelation of the Holy Spirit, every reader will find the faith to overcome and the keys to living the victorious life in Jesus Christ.

Reverend Joanne Moody
Agape Freedom Fighters
Agape Apostolic Equipping and Training Center, LIFE School
@revjoannemoody

introduction

THIS book is about the importance of soul detoxing, a concept that goes beyond religious doctrine and touches the very core of our well-being. It's like when we take a moment to cleanse our bodies, but this time, it's all about cleansing our inner selves – our souls.

IN the hustle and bustle of our lives, we often find ourselves caught in the whirlwind of emotions and stress. We tend to blame external factors for our emotional turmoil, but what if I told you that sometimes, it's our own souls that need a little cleansing? Just as we detox our bodies to get rid of the toxins we accumulate from unhealthy eating habits, our souls can also accumulate burdens and emotional baggage over time.

PICTURE this: you're on a journey of self-discovery, just like when you decide to eat healthier to improve your physical health. You're digging deep into your emotional well-being, realizing that the stuff you've been carrying around – those unresolved emotions, past hurts, and negative thoughts – can weigh you down, much like toxins in the body.

REMEMBER the moment when you started reading food labels and were astonished by what you found? It's similar when we begin to unravel the layers of our souls. We might uncover hidden hurts, grudges, or unresolved issues we've been carrying, and it can be eye-opening. Just as you learned to make healthier food choices, you can learn to make healthier emotional and spiritual choices too.

As someone who's been on a journey of self-discovery and wellness, I can tell you that understanding the importance of soul detoxing was a game-changer for me. It was like the lightbulb moment when you realize that what you put into your body matters. The same goes for what you allow into your soul.

THINK of your soul as the core of your being. Just as you'd nurture your body with the right nutrients, your soul also needs care and attention. It's not just about pointing fingers at external factors; it's about taking responsibility for our own well-being. We often forget that we are complex beings, composed of mind, body, and soul, and each aspect deserves our care.

IN today's fast-paced world, it's easy to get swept up in the chaos and forget to take care of ourselves. We blame external circumstances, our busy lives, or other people for how we feel. But, in reality, we have the power to nurture our souls and find the peace we seek. It's about quieting the inner turmoil and giving ourselves the space to detox emotionally, just as we detox our bodies physically. So, my friends, let's embark on this journey together. Just as we make choices to improve our physical health, we can make choices to enhance our emotional and spiritual well-being. Soul detoxing is not about religious doctrine; it's about personal growth and finding inner peace. Join me as we explore ways to cleanse our souls, let go of emotional baggage, and embrace a more balanced and harmonious life. Remember, taking care of your soul is an essential part of self-care, and you're worth it.

week one

Day 1

Self-Care: Nurturing Your Mind, Body, and Spirit

An issue that weighs heavily on most of us is self-love. I had a phone call with my daughter recently, and we were discussing Whitney Houston's song, "The Greatest Love of All" (if you haven't heard it, I highly recommend giving it a listen). But you know what? While that song talks about self-love, the greatest love truly comes from the Lord. However, self-love is also incredibly important. Often, we pour out our love onto others, which is beautiful, but we tend to forget about loving ourselves. This oversight can lead us into situations where we inadvertently reject ourselves emotionally.

We may not even realize it, but sometimes we search for reasons to believe that people will reject us. We question whether they'll reject our message, our personalities, our very being, or even our presence in certain places. So, I'd like to encourage all of you to take a moment to pause and reflect. If you have a journal, this is a great time to do some journaling.

Start by jotting down three things:

> How do I express love for the Lord?

DAY 1

> How do I show love for myself?

> How do I demonstrate love for other people?

Now, take a good look at how much time you spend on each of these aspects. Do you have a balance? I can imagine that for many of us, that balance might be way off. Are you dedicating time to your relationship with Jesus? Are you attending church? Are you reading the Word? If you haven't started, remember that your relationship with the Lord is the most important thing; everything else hinges on it. But I believe you're reading this because you already have a relationship with the Lord. So, let me ask, do you have a relationship with yourself?

THERE'S an old saying that goes, "self-care isn't selfish," and it holds so much truth. We often emphasize pouring out love for

DAY 1

others, which is fantastic, but we forget that we also need to replenish ourselves. Self-care is a crucial part of this equation. How do you love yourself? Are you allowing yourself the rest you deserve? There are seasons in life that demand more from us, like when I was a new mom and getting enough sleep felt like a luxury. But let me assure you, sleep will eventually return for those of you with little ones. Some of us, however, don't allow ourselves enough rest. We keep pushing ourselves to go, go, go.

I REMEMBER a moment when the Lord said something profound to me:

> "IF I, THE CREATOR OF THE UNIVERSE, CHOSE TO TAKE A SABBATH DAY AND REST, WHO DO YOU THINK YOU ARE TO BELIEVE YOU DON'T NEED IT?"

I can guarantee you that God didn't rest on the seventh day because He was tired. He rested to set a precedent that we need rest and self-care. So, this week, I want to challenge you to journal about your self-care routine and resting habits.

CONSIDER THESE QUESTIONS:

What do you do to rest?

How are you resting?

How are you taking care of yourself?

DAY 1

ALWAYS REMEMBER: how can you care for others if you don't care for yourself? You've probably heard flight attendants say on airplanes, "In case of an emergency, put on your oxygen mask before assisting your child." As a mom, that might sound unbelievable; you'd want to protect your child at all costs. But think about it, what if your brain isn't getting enough oxygen? You won't be able to help your child effectively. You need to oxygenate your mind so you can think clearly and efficiently.

ARE there areas in your life where you're not achieving your goals at the rate, quality, or quantity you should be? Perhaps it's because you're not taking proper care of yourself; your body, your mind, and your spirit might be in survival mode. But remember, we're not meant to merely survive; we're meant to thrive, and we can't thrive without rest.

HERE'S SOMETHING TO PONDER: if you were to run a marathon, you'd know that the next day, your body would need nothing but rest. But what about your mind? Are you constantly thinking about what needs to be done next? Are you giving your mind the rest it deserves, those quiet moments for deep breaths and just being still?

THIS WEEK, reflect on how you can love yourself better:

> How will you care for yourself?

> What can you improve in your self-care routine?

> What can you remove or add to your life to ensure self-care?

FOR EXAMPLE, I had to start taking vitamins, even though I didn't like it. I also had to cut back on my favorite indulgence: crispy, greasy french fries. They weren't good for my body, so I had to make a change.

THINK about what you need to eliminate from your life to love yourself more and what you need to add. Remember what the Bible says in Ephesians: we are God's masterpiece. He loves us and created us to be the best version of ourselves. He cares for you, and we need to care for ourselves in return.

Consider these questions:

> How are you nurturing your soul, mind, and will?

> How are you tending to your spirit?

> Are you reading the Bible, praying, or journaling?

> How are you treating your body?

> Are you giving it the care it deserves?

THIS WEEK, let's focus on loving ourselves to the fullest, because if you are His masterpiece, then He desires for you to be well-cared for, mind, body and soul,

DAY 1

It's time to love yourself, just as Ephesians 2:10 encourages us. How do you love yourself, mind, body, and spirit?

Day 2

. . .

Devotion 1: Loving Yourself as God's Masterpiece

SCRIPTURE:

> *EPHESIANS 2:10 (NIV) - "FOR WE ARE GOD'S MASTERPIECE. HE HAS CREATED US ANEW IN CHRIST JESUS, SO WE CAN DO THE GOOD THINGS HE PLANNED FOR US LONG AGO."*

IN THIS VERSE, we are reminded that we are God's masterpiece, created with purpose and intention. Just as an artist carefully crafts a masterpiece, God designed us with great care. Our Creator loves us deeply and desires us to care for ourselves in the same way.

> ***Reflection:*** *Take a moment to reflect on this truth. Begin by praying and thanking God for creating you as His masterpiece. Consider the ways in which you can show love and care for yourself, both physically and spiritually. Journal your thoughts on how you can better love yourself, just as God loves you.*
>
> ***Action:*** *Make a commitment to incorporate self-care into your daily routine. Whether it's dedicating time for prayer and reflection,*

DAY 2

setting aside moments for physical rest, or making healthier choices in your life, remember that taking care of yourself is an act of worship to the One who designed you.

TAKE a little break and jot down your thoughts on what you've read so far in your journal. It's a great way to process and internalize what you've read so far.

___

___

___

___

___

___

___

DAY 2

. . .

D^{AY 3}

Devotion 2: Balancing Self-Care and Service

SCRIPTURE:

> MATTHEW 22:39 (NIV) - "LOVE YOUR NEIGHBOR AS YOURSELF."

THE BIBLE TEACHES us to love our neighbors as ourselves. This implies that self-love and love for others are interconnected. To truly love others, we must first love ourselves. Neglecting self-care can hinder our ability to serve and love those around us effectively.

> **Reflection:** *Begin by meditating on the importance of self-love as a foundation for loving others. Pray for guidance on finding the balance between self-care and service to others. Journal your thoughts on how this balance can be achieved in your life.*
>
> **Action:** *Commit to a week of intentional self-care. Create a self-care plan that includes time for rest, reflection, and activities that nourish your body, mind, and spirit. As you experience the benefits of self-love, you'll be better equipped to love and serve others.*

DAY 3

. . .

TAKE a moment to reflect on what you've read up to this point and write down your thoughts in your journal. This can help you better grasp and absorb the information.

_____

_____

_____

_____

_____

_____

_____

. . .

DAY 3

D^{ay 4}

. . .

Devotion 3: Restoring Your Spirit Through Self-Care

Scripture:

> Psalm 23:2-3 (NIV) - He makes me lie down in green pastures, he leads me beside quiet waters, he refreshes my soul.

Psalm 23 reminds us of the restorative power of God's care. Just as a shepherd leads his sheep to peaceful pastures and quiet waters, God wants to refresh our souls through self-care. It's not selfish; it's necessary for our spiritual well-being.

Reflection: Spend time in prayer, reflecting on Psalm 23 and God's desire to refresh your soul. Consider the areas in your life where you may be neglecting self-care and the impact it has on your spirit. Journal your thoughts and feelings.

Action: This week, make a deliberate effort to incorporate self-care practices that nurture your spirit. Set aside time for prayer, meditation, or reading Scripture. Seek moments of stillness and tranquility in your daily routine. As you do, you'll experience the restorative

DAY 4

power of self-care and draw closer to God's loving presence.

PAUSE AND USE your journal to capture your thoughts on what you've read thus far. It's an effective way to gain a deeper understanding of the material.

. . .

DAY 4

Day 5

Put What You've Learned in to Action

I ENCOURAGE you to take a moment for prayerful reflection on the guidance provided and journal your thoughts on how you can integrate these principles into your daily life. Seek spiritual clarity and direction, and through prayer, chart a course to apply these teachings in a way that aligns with your faith and values. This introspective practice can lead to meaningful growth and transformation in your journey.

I ENCOURAGE you to take a moment for prayerful reflection on the guidance provided and journal your thoughts on how you can integrate these principles into your daily life. Seek spiritual clarity and direction, and through prayer, chart a course to apply these teachings in a way that aligns with your faith and values. This introspective practice can lead to meaningful growth and transformation in your journey.

Here are five self-care tips to help you prioritize your well-being and maintain a healthy balance in your life:

Practice Mindful Moments:

- Spend a few minutes each day in mindful meditation. Find a quiet space, sit comfortably, and focus on your breath and sensations in your body. Mindfulness meditation can help reduce stress, improve focus, and promote emotional well-being.

Establish Healthy Boundaries:

- Learn to set boundaries in your personal and professional life. Saying "no" when necessary and creating space for your needs is essential for maintaining a healthy balance. Boundaries protect your time and energy, allowing you to prioritize self-care.

Regular Physical Activity:

- Engage in regular physical activity that you enjoy, whether it's yoga, jogging, dancing, or simply taking long walks. Exercise not only benefits your physical health but also releases endorphins, reducing stress and enhancing your mood.

Unplug from Technology:

- Set aside designated times each day to disconnect from your devices, especially before bedtime. The constant exposure to screens can disrupt sleep patterns and contribute to stress. Use this time to unwind, read, or engage in offline hobbies.

Nurture Your Passions and Interests:

- Make time for activities that bring you joy and fulfillment. Whether it's painting, writing, gardening, or any other hobby, immersing yourself in what you love can be a source of relaxation and creativity.

REMEMBER that self-care is a personal journey, and it's essential to tailor your self-care practices to your unique needs and preferences. Prioritizing self-care allows you to recharge, reduce stress, and ultimately lead a more balanced and fulfilling life.

SELFCARE Checklist

	M	T	W	TH	F	SA	SU
Spend some time in prayer to start the day	☐	☐	☐	☐	☐	☐	☐
Enjoy 45 minutes of exercise	☐	☐	☐	☐	☐	☐	☐
Get some fresh air	☐	☐	☐	☐	☐	☐	☐
Have a healthy breakfast	☐	☐	☐	☐	☐	☐	☐
Enjoy a warm morning drink	☐	☐	☐	☐	☐	☐	☐
Plan out your day in your planner	☐	☐	☐	☐	☐	☐	☐
Stretch your body	☐	☐	☐	☐	☐	☐	☐
Take regular breaks	☐	☐	☐	☐	☐	☐	☐
Enjoy some sunshine	☐	☐	☐	☐	☐	☐	☐
Take hot/Cold bath or shower	☐	☐	☐	☐	☐	☐	☐
Read something meaningful	☐	☐	☐	☐	☐	☐	☐
Play some invigorating music	☐	☐	☐	☐	☐	☐	☐
Disconnect	☐	☐	☐	☐	☐	☐	☐
Eat a healthy snack	☐	☐	☐	☐	☐	☐	☐
Wind down by avoiding bright light at night	☐	☐	☐	☐	☐	☐	☐
Get in bed before 10pm	☐	☐	☐	☐	☐	☐	☐

week two

DAY 6

Renewal Through Balance: Embracing God's Presence in Daily Life

I CHERISH those bright and sunny mornings when I can simply sit on my patio, basking in the warmth of the sun on my face and feeling the gentle caress of a breeze on my skin. It's during these moments that I can tangibly and peacefully experience the presence of the Lord. My dear friend, who happens to be a certified fitness instructor, once told me that spending just three minutes facing the morning sun can do wonders for your mood, hormone balance, and energy levels. Just think about it – if the sun can do that for our physical bodies, imagine what sitting in the presence of God every morning can do for our lives!

SOMETIMES, we tend to overlook the incredible benefits of simply being in the presence of the Lord. It's not always easy to do, is it? I know many of you may find it a bit challenging just thinking about it. Our busy schedules and daily responsibilities can easily distract us. Family and parenting duties can make us feel like we need to keep moving. Our minds may start racing, and our bodies might even become a tad restless when we attempt to sit still. And for those of you who struggle with sleep, you might find yourself nodding off pretty quickly. We all have our own unique challenges, but let's not forget what the Scriptures tell us:

DAY 6

 "Be still and know that I am God."

OUR FAST-PACED LIVES, the desire to keep up with our neighbors, and the pursuit of that perfect career can sometimes make us forget that being in the presence of the Lord can make us better spouses, parents, friends, and employees.

WHEN WE TAKE the time to quiet ourselves down and allow the Lord's presence to envelop us, we make room for His promises to be revealed. The peace that surpasses all understanding guards our hearts and minds in Christ Jesus (Philippians 4:7). When we spend time in God's presence, we can cast our worries and concerns upon Him, trusting that He will accomplish all that He desires in our lives.

SO, I encourage you to give it a try. Start with baby steps today. As time goes on, you'll find yourself able to sit in His presence for longer periods. Here are some simple steps to get you started:

FIND A QUIET PLACE.

> *Turn off your electronics (yes, you can do it, even if it's just for a few minutes).*
>
> *Invite the Holy Spirit to join you.*
> *Sit quietly for just three minutes.*

How did you feel during those moments?

Take this opportunity to open your heart and share your thoughts and feelings with the Lord.

___

___

___

___

___

___

___

___

. . .

DAY 6

Day 7

. . .

Devotional 1: "Embracing the Morning Light"

SCRIPTURE:

> Psalm 143:8 (NIV) - "Let the morning bring me word of your unfailing love, for I have put my trust in you. Show me the way I should go, for to you I entrust my life."

Reflection: As the sun rises and bathes the world in its warm light, take a moment to sit in its presence. Just like the sun can positively affect our mood and energy, spending time in the presence of the Lord in the morning can illuminate our day. It's a time when we can trust Him with our lives and seek His guidance. In the stillness of the morning, open your heart to God's unfailing love, and let Him show you the way forward.

Prayer: Heavenly Father, as I embrace the morning light, I entrust my life to You. May Your unfailing love guide me today, and may I find strength and direction in Your presence. In Jesus' name, I pray. Amen.

DAY 7

You can benefit from taking some time to journal your thoughts about what you've read so far. This simple practice can help you better digest and comprehend the information.

_____

_____

_____

_____

_____

_____

_____

_____

. . .

DAY 7

D^{AY 8}

Devotional 2: "Be Still and Know"

SCRIPTURE:

> PSALM 46:10 (NIV) - "BE STILL, AND KNOW THAT I AM GOD; I WILL BE EXALTED AMONG THE NATIONS, I WILL BE EXALTED IN THE EARTH."

Reflection: *In the hustle and bustle of life, finding time to be still can be challenging. Yet, God's Word reminds us of the importance of stillness and knowing that He is God. Just as we take a moment to sit quietly before the sun rises, let's also take time to be in God's presence. When we are still, we make room for Him to be exalted in our lives and to speak to our hearts.*

Prayer: *Lord, in the midst of my busy life, help me to find moments of stillness with You. I want to know You more deeply and experience Your presence. Be exalted in my heart and in all the earth. In Jesus' name, I pray. Amen.*

DAY 8

I ENCOURAGE you to set aside a moment to write down your reflections on what you've read until now. Journaling can enhance your understanding of the material.

———

. . .

DAY 8

Day 9

. . .

Devotional 3: "Growing in His Presence"

SCRIPTURE:

> PSALM 92:12-14 (NIV) - "THE RIGHTEOUS WILL FLOURISH LIKE A PALM TREE, THEY WILL GROW LIKE A CEDAR OF LEBANON; PLANTED IN THE HOUSE OF THE LORD, THEY WILL FLOURISH IN THE COURTS OF OUR GOD. THEY WILL STILL BEAR FRUIT IN OLD AGE, THEY WILL STAY FRESH AND GREEN."

REFLECTION: Just as a palm tree and a cedar grow strong and flourish when planted in the right environment, we too can flourish when we are planted in the presence of the Lord. As we spend time with Him, we grow spiritually, bear fruit in every season of life, and remain fresh and green. Today, make an effort to sit in His presence, knowing that in His company, you are continually growing and becoming more like Him.

PRAYER: Gracious God, I desire to flourish in Your presence and become more like You each day. Plant me firmly in Your house, and may I bear fruit that brings glory to Your name. Thank You for the opportunity to grow in Your love and grace. In Jesus' name, I pray. Amen.

. . .

DAY 9

ALLOCATE some time to journal your thoughts on the material you've covered so far. This can aid in your comprehension and retention of the information.

___

. . .

DAY 9

Day 10

Put What You've Learned into Action

TODAY'S OBJECTIVE is to integrate the wisdom you've acquired this week, incorporating biblical teachings and scripture into your daily life. Utilize the provided guidance to contemplate this chapter, aligning it with your faith, and strategize how to put it into practice. Remember the biblical references, such as Proverbs 2:6-7 and James 1:22, which emphasize the importance of seeking wisdom, taking action, and trusting in the Lord. Journal your commitment to actively live out these principles, recognizing the path they illuminate on your spiritual journey.

Here are five tips for embracing a balanced and renewing life:

DAY 10

1. *Morning Ritual of Stillness:*

- Begin your day with a few minutes of stillness. Find a quiet spot, sit in the morning sunlight, and invite the presence of the Lord into your heart. This simple morning ritual can set a positive tone for your day, boost your mood, and provide guidance for the challenges ahead.

2. *Prioritize Quiet Time:*

- In our fast-paced world, make an intentional effort to prioritize quiet time with God. Schedule moments of stillness in your daily routine, whether it's early in the morning, during a lunch break, or before bedtime. Disconnect from electronics and create a sacred space for reflection and prayer.

3. Balancing Growth and Rest:

- Recognize that growth and rest are interconnected. Just as you exercise your body and mind, allow yourself time for rest and recovery. Similarly, in your spiritual journey, balance the pursuit of spiritual virtues with moments of rest and abiding in God's presence. This equilibrium promotes overall well-being.

4. Be Present in God's Presence:

- When you sit in the presence of the Lord, be fully present. Release your worries, concerns, and distractions, and open your heart to Him. Use this time to share your thoughts, feelings, and desires with God. Let His peace fill your heart and mind.

5. Start Small, Grow Steadily:

- If you find it challenging to sit still in God's presence initially, remember that growth takes time. Begin with just a few minutes each day and gradually increase the duration as you become more comfortable. Over time, you'll develop a deeper connection with God through these moments of stillness.

week three

Day 11

Embracing Authenticity: Finding Purpose Beyond Comparison and Competition

STOP COMPARING AND COMPETING WITH OTHERS

I'VE SPENT TOO much time trying to be like other people, and it never left me feeling happy or content. Instead, it led to constant striving, pressure, and self-doubt. We were designed to stand out, not to blend in. As P.T. Barnum once stated, "No one ever made a difference by being like everyone else." This truth resonates with us because we were created for a unique purpose that only we can fulfill. When we spend our time trying to be someone we're not, we'll never reach the potential that God has for us.

WE ALL HIDE behind different things—some behind their musical gifts, athletic talents, and others behind the accomplishments of others. But regardless of the façade, we hide. Why do we do this? Once again, it varies for each of us; there are countless reasons. It's far easier to deny our feelings of insecurity than to confront them head-on. Who really wants to deal with the skeletons in their closet? Most of us would prefer to bar the door shut, lock it, and lose the key.

DAY 11

However, the root of our issue lies in our flawed belief system. We erroneously think that people around us have it all together while we're the only ones who fall short of certain criteria. We convince ourselves that we'll never quite measure up or be good enough. So, what do we do? We put on a mask and start to hide. We try to look the part, pretending that we're not hurting and that we don't need help. We put on a show, acting like things don't matter, and striving to convince people that we're okay.

This pattern starts at a very early age. We seek the approval of family, friends, and, surprisingly, even our enemies. We desperately want to fit in or feel accepted, so we're willing to change who we are or hide who we are to fit in. Sadly, while we're working so hard to look right, we often neglect to work on getting right emotionally. It's time to take off the mask.

Yes, we're flawed. Yes, we make mistakes, and yes, we don't always meet the standard. However, despite all of this, we are loved, accepted, and forgiven.

The Bible is full of stories of people who didn't meet the standards of their day. They were murderers, adulterers, liars, and cheats who were forced to confront their true selves. They knew they weren't worthy of God's love or favor, but they discovered the transformative power of God's grace. They stopped letting their past hurts and experiences be their crutch and allowed them to become their wings.

It's okay to be yourself; no one expects perfection. We're all in the battle, striving to become the best versions of ourselves. Just

DAY 11

remember, it takes the power of the Holy Spirit to heal the hurts you've been hiding inside, but it also requires you to take off the mask.

Day 12

. . .

Devotion 1: "Breaking Free from Comparison and Competition"

SCRIPTURE:

> ROMANS 12:2 - "DO NOT CONFORM TO THE PATTERN OF THIS WORLD, BUT BE TRANSFORMED BY THE RENEWING OF YOUR MIND."

Reflection: *Today, let's reflect on the wisdom shared in the document about the dangers of comparing ourselves to others and competing to fit in. The world often pressures us to conform to its standards, leaving us feeling inadequate and insecure. But as followers of Christ, we are called to a higher purpose. We are uniquely designed and loved by God.*

Prayer: *Heavenly Father, help us break free from the destructive patterns of comparison and competition. Renew our minds and hearts, reminding us of our unique purpose in your kingdom. May we find contentment in being the individuals you created us to be. In Jesus' name, we pray. Amen.*

I RECOMMEND that you take a moment to record your thoughts about the content you've gone through. Journaling can enhance your grasp of the material.

DAY 12

. . .

D^{ay 13}

...

Devotion 2: "Removing the Masks"

SCRIPTURE:

> PSALM 139:14 - "I PRAISE YOU BECAUSE I AM FEARFULLY AND WONDERFULLY MADE; YOUR WORKS ARE WONDERFUL, I KNOW THAT FULL WELL."

Reflection: *In this devotion, let's focus on the idea of taking off the masks we wear to hide our insecurities and imperfections. God fearfully and wonderfully made each of us, and there's no need to pretend to be someone else. We are loved, accepted, and forgiven just as we are.*

Prayer: *Gracious God, help us to remove the masks we wear and be authentic in our faith journey. Remind us that we are wonderfully made by your hand. Grant us the courage to embrace our flaws and vulnerabilities, knowing that your love covers all. In Jesus' name, we pray. Amen.*

TAKE a little break and jot down your thoughts on what you've read so far in your journal. It's a great way to process and understand the information better.

Day 14

Devotion 3: "Embracing God's Transforming Grace"

SCRIPTURE:

> 2 Corinthians 12:9 - "But he said to me, 'My grace is sufficient for you, for my power is made perfect in weakness.'"

Reflection: *Today's devotion focuses on embracing God's transforming grace. We may have made mistakes and felt unworthy, but God's grace is sufficient to heal and strengthen us. Just like the individuals in the Bible who found redemption despite their imperfections, we too can experience transformation through God's grace.*

Prayer: *Heavenly Father, thank you for your abundant grace that is sufficient for us in our weaknesses. Help us to fully embrace your transformative power in our lives. May we find hope and healing in your grace and be a light to others who are still hiding behind their masks. In Jesus' name, we pray. Amen.*

Take a moment to reflect on what you've read up to this point and write down your thoughts in your journal. This can help you better grasp and absorb the information.

DAY 14

D^{ay 15}

Put What You've Learned into Action

SET ASIDE some dedicated time for prayer and contemplation as you carefully consider the tips offered. In your journal, map out concrete ways to implement these valuable insights into your everyday life. Through this prayerful reflection and thoughtful planning, you can bring these principles to life in a manner that resonates deeply with your faith and convictions, fostering personal growth and spiritual enrichment.

Here are five helpful tips to help you stop comparing and competing with others:

DAY 15

1. Embrace Your Uniqueness:

- Recognize that you are fearfully and wonderfully made by God. Embrace your individuality and the unique gifts and talents that set you apart from others.
- Tip: Spend time in self-reflection and prayer to discover and appreciate your unique qualities. Make a list of your strengths and qualities that make you special.

2. Focus on Personal Growth:

- Shift your focus from trying to fit in or meet external standards to personal growth and self-improvement.
- Tip: Set specific, achievable goals for yourself and work towards them. Celebrate your progress, no matter how small the steps may seem.

3. Seek Authentic Relationships:

- Surround yourself with people who accept you for who you are and encourage your personal growth. Avoid relationships built on competition or comparison.
- Tip: Nurture deep and authentic connections with friends and loved ones. Share your thoughts and

feelings openly with those who support and uplift you.

4. Practice Vulnerability:

- Be willing to be vulnerable and authentic about your struggles and insecurities. It's okay to admit when you're not okay.
- Tip: Find a trusted friend or mentor with whom you can share your thoughts and feelings honestly. Opening up can be a powerful step towards healing.

5. Lean on God's Grace:

- Trust in God's grace and forgiveness. Remember that God's love is unconditional and that His grace covers your imperfections.
- Tip: Spend time in prayer and meditation on scriptures that emphasize God's grace and love. When you feel the urge to compare or compete, turn to God for strength and reassurance.

THESE TIPS ARE DESIGNED to help you break free from the cycle of comparison and competition and instead focus on personal growth, authenticity, and a deeper connection with God and others.

week four

D^{AY 16}

Balancing Compassion and Responsibility: A Guide to Navigating Life's Dramas

I'VE ALWAYS BEEN a compassionate person. I can't even watch a movie without feeling the pain of the main character. If they get hurt, I feel a pang in my chest. I genuinely cherish this aspect of myself, as it reflects the empathy that the Lord has placed in my heart. However, there have been times when this empathy has weighed me down.

MANY TIMES, I found myself listening to a friend or a fellow congregant sharing a traumatic experience. I would become so consumed by anger or disgust towards the perpetrator that I felt just as offended as the victim. Nights were spent worrying about their feelings. Thankfully, I usually didn't know or have contact with the wrongdoers because I'm not sure if I would have been able to walk in grace and forgiveness if I did.

THROUGH THESE EXPERIENCES, I have a few valuable lessons that I'd like to share with you today.

FIRST, the Bible teaches us in Galatians 6:2 to

DAY 16

> Carry each other's burdens, and in this way, you will fulfill the law of Christ."

This verse reminds us of our duty to support one another during trying times. However, it's essential to discern whose burdens we should bear. In 1 Peter 5:7, we are encouraged to

> Cast all our anxieties on Him because He cares for us."

This implies that we should turn to the Lord for our own concerns and invite others to do the same.

WE ENCOUNTER people in our lives who seem to thrive on chaos, turning every moment into a three-ring circus. They may not feel normal unless there's constant drama around them. During such moments, we must ask ourselves, "Whose circus is this?" As mentioned in Matthew 7:3, "Why do you look at the speck of sawdust in your brother's eye and pay no attention to the plank in your own eye?" Let us focus on managing our own affairs before trying to solve someone else's problems.

REMEMBER the story of Martha and Mary in Luke 10:38-42. Martha was burdened with serving, while Mary chose to sit at the Lord's feet and listen. Jesus said, "Mary has chosen what is better." Sometimes, choosing what is better means not getting caught up in other people's dramas but rather encouraging them to seek the Lord's guidance.

IT'S crucial to be compassionate and supportive without allowing someone else's drama to consume us. Galatians 6:5 says,

"For each will have to bear his own load." We do a disservice to ourselves and our friends when we carry their burdens instead of helping them learn to carry them independently.

Let's strive to be stars in our own three-ring circus, as 2 Corinthians 10:12 advises us not to compare ourselves with others. While we should be there for our friends and loved ones, let us also remember to direct them towards God, the ultimate problem solver and source of peace.

D^{ay 17}

Devotional 1: Bearing Each Other's Burdens

SCRIPTURE:

> GALATIANS 6:2 (NIV) - "CARRY EACH OTHER'S BURDENS, AND IN THIS WAY, YOU WILL FULFILL THE LAW OF CHRIST."

IN OUR JOURNEY OF FAITH, we are called to be compassionate and supportive towards one another. Galatians 6:2 reminds us of this important duty. It encourages us to "carry each other's burdens." But, as we learned in our previous message, it's equally vital to discern whose burdens we should bear.

> ***Reflection:*** *Let us ponder on this today: Who in your life needs your support and encouragement? Whose burdens can you help carry? Remember, when we do this, we fulfill the law of Christ, walking in His footsteps of love and compassion.*

> ***Prayer:*** *Dear Lord, help us to be discerning in our compassion, to know when to carry others' burdens and when to direct them to You. May we fulfill the law of Christ by supporting and loving one another as You have loved us. In Jesus' name, we pray. Amen.*

DAY 17

· · ·

Pause and use your journal to capture your thoughts on what you've read thus far. It's an effective way to gain a deeper understanding of the material.

· · ·

DAY 17

Day 18

Devotional 2: Choosing What Is Better

SCRIPTURE:

> LUKE 10:42 (NIV) - "MARY HAS CHOSEN WHAT IS BETTER, AND IT WILL NOT BE TAKEN AWAY FROM HER."

IN LUKE 10:42, we read about Mary choosing to sit at the Lord's feet and listen, while Martha busied herself with serving. Jesus commended Mary for choosing what is better. Sometimes, we need to make choices that prioritize our spiritual well-being over getting entangled in the drama of life.

> ***Reflection:*** *Today, consider this: Are there moments when you need to prioritize spending time with the Lord, seeking His guidance, and finding peace in His presence, rather than getting caught up in the chaos around you?*
>
> ***Prayer:*** *Lord, help us to choose what is better, to seek Your presence, and find rest in Your wisdom and grace. May we be guided by Your Spirit in making decisions that align with Your will. In Jesus' name, we pray. Amen.*

DAY 18

You can benefit from taking some time to journal your thoughts about what you've read so far. This simple practice can help you better digest and comprehend the information.

___

___

___

___

___

___

___

___

. . .

DAY 18

Day 19

Devotional 3: Carrying Our Own Load

SCRIPTURE:

> GALATIANS 6:5 (NIV) - "FOR EACH WILL HAVE TO BEAR HIS OWN LOAD."

GALATIANS 6:5 reminds us that while we are called to carry one another's burdens, each of us also has our own load to bear. It's important to find the balance between supporting others and taking responsibility for our own lives.

> ***Reflection:*** *As you reflect on this verse, consider: Are there areas in your life where you need to take more ownership and responsibility? Are there burdens you should lay at the feet of the Lord, seeking His guidance and strength?*
>
> ***Prayer:*** *Heavenly Father, grant us the wisdom to discern when to carry others' burdens and when to rely on Your strength for our own. Help us to find balance and peace in our journey of faith. In Jesus' name, we pray. Amen.*

I ENCOURAGE you to set aside a moment to write down your reflections on what you've read until now. Journaling can enhance your understanding of the material.

DAY 19

. . .

D^{AY 20}

. . .

Put What You Learned into Action

TAKE a moment to pause and engage in prayerful reflection, delving into the practical tips provided. In your journal, sketch out a roadmap for how you intend to incorporate these insightful lessons into your daily life. By merging your contemplative spirit and strategic planning, you can activate these principles in ways that resonate with your personal faith and beliefs, fostering growth and spiritual enrichment.

Here's 5 Helpful tips to balance Compassion and Responsibility

1. Encourage Independence:

- Instead of always being the problem solver for others, encourage them to seek God's guidance and find solutions independently. Support their growth and self-reliance, guiding them to trust in the Lord.

2. Trust God's Grace:

- Understand that you may not always have the capacity to forgive or walk in grace as Mary did. Trust in God's grace and forgiveness, and remember that it's okay to seek His help when faced with challenging situations or difficult people.

BY FOLLOWING THESE TIPS, you can navigate the complexities of compassion, responsibility, and faith in a balanced and meaningful way.

week five

Day 21

Surround Yourself with Vision and Ideas, Not Gossip

HAVE you ever noticed how the company you keep can really shape who you become? It's like that saying – we're the sum of the five people we spend the most time with. Now, I can't pinpoint where I first heard this wisdom, or if it's even officially documented, but it sure makes you think, doesn't it?

I MEAN, think about it for a moment. We all have those friends or acquaintances who seem to thrive on talking about other people's lives and drama. But here's the thing: our time is precious, and we can choose how to spend it. Instead of getting caught up in discussions about others, why not invest that energy in creating the life you truly want to live?

AND IN THE book of Proverbs, it reminds us, "Whoever walks with the wise becomes wise, but the companion of fools will suffer harm." (Proverbs 13:20, ESV). So, I pay close attention to the people in my life. I watch how they behave, listen to the conversations they engage in, and observe how they react to those around them. Why? Because I want to surround myself with folks who inspire me, who share ideas and visions, and who uplift and encourage one another.

. . .

DAY 21

Now, I'm all about positivity and personal growth, and that's why I've made a conscious choice. If someone in my circle isn't reflecting the kind of person I aspire to be, I limit my time with them. It's not about cutting people out entirely, but it's about preserving my emotional well-being.

I GENUINELY WANT to make a positive impact on the lives of those around me, and in Ephesians 4:29, it says, "Let no corrupting talk come out of your mouths, but only such as is good for building up, as fits the occasion, that it may give grace to those who hear." So, I can't let their negativity or gossip bring me down. It can be a delicate balance, for sure, but my emotional health matters to me, and I'm determined to protect it. After all, we have this one life to live, so let's make it count by surrounding ourselves with positivity, vision, and ideas.

Day 22

* * *

Devotion 1: Choosing Your Inner Circle

SCRIPTURE:

> PROVERBS 13:20 (ESV) - "WHOEVER WALKS WITH THE WISE BECOMES WISE, BUT THE COMPANION OF FOOLS WILL SUFFER HARM."

IN OUR DAILY walk with God, we are reminded of the importance of the company we keep. The wisdom found in Proverbs 13:20 emphasizes that those we surround ourselves with have a profound impact on our lives. Just as the people you spend the most time with shape who you become, they can also influence your spiritual journey.

> **Reflection:** *Take a moment to reflect on the people you spend the most time with. Are they wise and uplifting, or do they engage in negativity and gossip? Consider how their presence affects your relationship with God. Today, let's pray for discernment to choose companions who inspire us on our spiritual journey.*
>
> **Prayer:** *Heavenly Father, help us choose companions who walk in Your wisdom, that we may be encouraged and strengthened in our faith. Guide us to be positive influences on others as well. In Jesus' name, we pray. Amen.*

DAY 22

ALLOCATE some time to journal your thoughts on the material you've covered so far. This can aid in your comprehension and retention of the information.

. . .

DAY 22

D^{AY 23}

. . .

Devotion 2: Guarding Your Emotional Health

SCRIPTURE:

> EPHESIANS 4:29 (ESV) - "LET NO CORRUPTING TALK COME OUT OF YOUR MOUTHS, BUT ONLY SUCH AS IS GOOD FOR BUILDING UP, AS FITS THE OCCASION, THAT IT MAY GIVE GRACE TO THOSE WHO HEAR."

IN EPHESIANS 4:29, we are reminded of the power of our words and the importance of guarding our emotional health. Engaging in gossip or negative talk not only harms others but also affects our own well-being. As followers of Christ, we are called to speak words that build up and bring grace to those around us.

> **Reflection:** *Reflect on your recent conversations. Have your words been a source of encouragement and grace, or have you engaged in gossip or negativity? Today, let's commit to using our words to uplift and encourage, in accordance with Ephesians 4:29.*
>
> **Prayer:** *Gracious God, help us to be mindful of our words, that we may bring grace and encouragement to others. Guard our hearts from negativity and gossip, and guide us in*

DAY 23

using our words for Your glory. In Jesus' name, we pray. Amen.

I RECOMMEND that you take a moment to record your thoughts about the content you've gone through. Journaling can enhance your grasp of the material.

_____

_____

_____

_____

_____

_____

_____

. . .

DAY 23

Day 24

Devotion 3: Creating a Life of Purpose

SCRIPTURE:

> JEREMIAH 29:11 (NIV) - "FOR I KNOW THE PLANS I HAVE FOR YOU, DECLARES THE LORD, PLANS FOR WELFARE AND NOT FOR EVIL, TO GIVE YOU A FUTURE AND A HOPE."

As we choose our inner circle and guard our emotional health, we are aligning ourselves with God's plan for our lives. Jeremiah 29:11 assures us that God has plans for our welfare and a future filled with hope. By surrounding ourselves with positive, visionary, and God-fearing individuals, we are better positioned to fulfill these divine plans.

> ***Reflection:*** *Consider the people in your life who reflect God's goodness and inspire you to live a life of purpose. How can you further nurture these relationships? How can you, in turn, be a positive influence on them? Today, let's pray for wisdom to cultivate these connections as we strive to fulfill God's plan for our lives.*
>
> ***Prayer:*** *Heavenly Father, thank You for the hope and purpose You provide. Bless our relationships and guide us in being positive influences on each other. May our lives be a testament to*

DAY 24

Your plans for our welfare. In Jesus' name, we pray. Amen.

D^{ay 25}

Put What You've Learned into Action

I INVITE you to carve out some quiet time for prayer and deep contemplation as you explore the practical advice presented. In your journal, sketch out your personalized plan for applying these wisdom nuggets to your everyday life. By blending heartfelt reflection with strategic intention, you can infuse these principles with the essence of your faith and values, facilitating growth and spiritual enrichment

Here are five helpful steps based on the information provided to help you make positive changes in your life:

1. Evaluate Your Inner Circle:

- Take a close look at the people you spend the most time with. Are they uplifting, supportive, and aligned with your values and goals? Identify those who bring positivity and encouragement into your life.

2. Reflect on Your Conversations:

- Pay attention to the nature of your conversations. Are they centered around gossip, negativity, or building others up? Make a conscious effort to engage in discussions that inspire, encourage, and reflect God's grace.

3. Set Boundaries:

- Understand that it's okay to set boundaries with people who engage in harmful behaviors or conversations. Limit your time with those who consistently bring negativity into your life to protect your emotional well-being.

4. Seek Out Positive Influences:

- Actively seek out individuals who align with your values and inspire personal growth. Join groups or communities that promote positivity, faith, and shared visions for a brighter future.

5. Be a Positive Influence:

- Remember that you can also positively impact others. Be intentional in your words and actions, striving to be a source of encouragement, kindness, and grace to those around you. Lead by example and reflect God's love in your interactions.

BY FOLLOWING THESE STEPS, you can create a more supportive and uplifting environment in your life, one that aligns with your faith and helps you grow into the person God intends you to be.

week six

Day 26

Finding Strength and Overcoming Self-Doubt through Faith

HAVE you ever found yourself grappling with self-doubt, comparing your abilities to others, and wondering if you'll ever measure up? Take heart, for we are not alone in this struggle. We all face moments when our inner critic seems to gain the upper hand. In these times, it's vital to turn to the wisdom of the Bible for guidance and inspiration.

ALLOW me to introduce you to my remarkable husband – a true renaissance man. Whether it's leading worship, preaching, conducting business affairs, or managing our home with precision and organization, he's a modern-day Solomon (minus the additional 699 wives and 300 concubines, of course!). At times, I've questioned why he chose to marry me. Can you relate to that feeling of inadequacy?

THE BIBLE TEACHES us that each of us is uniquely designed with different gifts and callings. In 1 Corinthians 12:4-6 (NIV), it states, "There are different kinds of gifts, but the same Spirit distributes them. There are different kinds of service, but the same Lord. There are different kinds of working, but in all of them and in everyone, it is the same God at work." We are not meant to be carbon copies of one another, and it's crucial to appreciate the talents and abilities of others while embracing our own.

DAY 26

. . .

ONE MEMORABLE MORNING, my youngest daughter fell ill, and I rushed to her side. After attending to her needs, I attempted to focus on my writing, only to find my creative wellspring had seemingly run dry. As I pondered my perceived shortcomings, it was time to prepare my husband's traditional New Year's meal, despite his Greek heritage (the fragrant sauerkraut made its annual appearance!). In the midst of these duties, my son joined me, feeling queasy from indulging in holiday treats. We found solace on the couch, and my kitchen responsibilities temporarily slipped from my mind.

UPON MY HUSBAND'S AWAKENING, he noticed the undone tasks and, truth be told, expressed his disappointment. In that moment, I felt an overwhelming sense of shame and self-doubt. However, I recalled the words of Romans 8:1 (NIV), which states, "Therefore, there is now no condemnation for those who are in Christ Jesus." Guilt says we've done something bad, but shame says we are bad. While I may have made some missteps that morning, I am not a terrible person. It was a valuable lesson in the power of negative self-talk.

NEGATIVE SELF-TALK, as described in 2 Corinthians 10:5 (NIV), can lead to doubting oneself and comparing oneself to others. It can also foster feelings of inadequacy and jealousy towards those around us. Instead of succumbing to these destructive thoughts, we must turn to Scripture for guidance and strength.

. . .

DAY 26

GALATIANS 1:10 (NIV) reminds us, "Am I now trying to win the approval of human beings, or of God? Or am I trying to please people? If I were still trying to please people, I would not be a servant of Christ." Our ultimate goal should be to please our Heavenly Father, not to constantly seek the approval of others.

AS WE NAVIGATE the challenges of life, from familial obligations to work-related stress and strained relationships, we must remember that our souls consist of three components: our mind, our emotions, and our willpower. Proverbs 4:23 (NIV) advises us to "Above all else, guard your heart, for everything you do flows from it." Our willpower, when fully surrendered to the Lord, becomes our most potent tool against negative thoughts and emotions.

IN PHILIPPIANS 4:13 (NIV), we find reassurance: "I can do all this through him who gives me strength." Challenges will continue to arise, and temptations will persist, but with a strong willpower submitted to the Lord, we can prevail.

TO HELP REGAIN control over my emotions, I turned to the following biblical declarations:

> My spirit is in submission to the Holy Spirit. I will be guided and directed by His divine purpose.

> My soul is in submission to my spirit.

DAY 26

> My emotions and mind are submitted to my will, and because my will is stronger than my emotions, it will dictate what thoughts I choose to dwell on.

DEAR FRIEND, you are not alone in your struggles. We all wrestle with self-doubt and comparison from time to time. But with faith in God's plan and the strength He provides, we can rise above our feelings of inadequacy and find peace and confidence in ourselves. Keep your eyes on Jesus, trust in His divine purpose, and remember that you are fearfully and wonderfully made (Psalm 139:14, NIV).

Day 27

Devotion 1: Embracing Your Unique Design

SCRIPTURE:

> 1 Corinthians 12:4-6 (NIV) - "There are different kinds of gifts, but the same Spirit distributes them. There are different kinds of service, but the same Lord. There are different kinds of working, but in all of them and in everyone, it is the same God at work."

Reflection: *Have you ever found yourself comparing your abilities to those of others, feeling like you'll never measure up? In the journey of life, it's easy to fall into the trap of self-doubt. However, today's scripture reminds us that God has uniquely designed each one of us with different gifts and purposes. Just as a jigsaw puzzle is incomplete without each piece, so is the body of Christ without our individual contributions.*

Take a moment to reflect on your own unique gifts and talents. Instead of comparing yourself to others, embrace the qualities that make you special in God's eyes. Remember that He has a

DAY 27

specific plan for your life, and your abilities, no matter how different they may be from others, are vital to fulfilling that plan.

Prayer: *Heavenly Father, thank You for designing me with unique gifts and talents. Help me to embrace my individuality and to use my abilities to glorify You and serve others. Teach me not to compare myself to others but to focus on fulfilling the purpose You have set before me. In Jesus' name, I pray. Amen.*

TAKE a moment to jot down what you've learned and how you can put these ideas into practice in your life.

_____

_____

_____

_____

_____

DAY 27

. . .

D^{ay 28}

Devotion 2: Overcoming Negative Self-Talk

SCRIPTURE:

> ROMANS 8:1 (NIV) - "THEREFORE, THERE IS NOW NO CONDEMNATION FOR THOSE WHO ARE IN CHRIST JESUS."

Reflection: Self-doubt can often lead to negative self-talk, causing us to feel inadequate and unworthy. But as followers of Christ, we are reminded in Romans 8:1 that there is no condemnation for those who belong to Jesus. Guilt says we've done something bad, but shame says we are bad. We must recognize the difference and refuse to allow shame to define our worth.

When negative thoughts start to creep in, remember that you are a child of God, loved and cherished by Him. Instead of dwelling on self-condemnation, focus on His grace and forgiveness. Pray for the strength to overcome negative self-talk and embrace the freedom that comes from being in Christ Jesus.

Prayer: Gracious Lord, I thank You for the

DAY 28

> *freedom from condemnation that I find in Jesus. Help me to silence the negative self-talk that tries to rob me of my confidence and joy. Fill me with Your love and assurance, reminding me of my true worth in Your eyes. In Jesus' name, I pray. Amen.*

TAKE a little break and jot down your thoughts on what you've read so far in your journal.

_____

_____

_____

_____

_____

_____

. . .

DAY 28

D^{ay 29}

. . .

Devotion 3: Surrendering to God's Willpower

SCRIPTURE:

"PHILIPPIANS 4:13 (NIV) - "I CAN DO ALL THIS THROUGH HIM WHO GIVES ME STRENGTH."

Reflection: *Life's challenges can often make us feel overwhelmed, misunderstood, or exhausted. In those moments, it's essential to remember that our strength comes from God. Philippians 4:13 reminds us that we can do all things through Christ who strengthens us.*

When you face trials or negative thoughts, surrender to God's willpower. Let His strength be your guide and source of endurance. Trust that He will equip you to overcome any obstacle. As you rely on His power, you'll find peace and confidence even in the most challenging circumstances.

Prayer: *Heavenly Father, I acknowledge my dependence on Your strength. In times of difficulty and self-doubt, I choose to surrender to Your willpower. Fill me with Your grace and courage to face life's challenges, knowing that I can do all things through Christ who* *strengthens me. In His mighty name, I pray. Amen.*

Take a moment to reflect on what you've read up to this point and write down your thoughts in your journal.

___

___

___

___

___

___

___

DAY 29

. . .

D^{AY 30}

Put What You've Learned into Action

I ENCOURAGE you to allocate a moment for quiet reflection and prayer, immersing yourself in the practical guidance shared. Within your journal, craft a blueprint detailing how you intend to weave these pearls of wisdom into your daily existence. Through this blend of mindful contemplation and strategic planning, you'll breathe life into these principles in a manner that resonates deeply with your faith, igniting personal growth and spiritual enrichment

Here are five helpful tips based on the this chapter help you overcome self-doubt and embrace your unique identity in Christ:

OVERCOMING SELF-DOUBT

1. Recognize Your Unique Design:

- Understand that God has uniquely designed you with specific gifts, talents, and a divine purpose. Rather than comparing yourself to others, embrace your individuality. Spend time in prayer and self-reflection to discover your strengths and how you can use them to serve God and others effectively.

2. Guard Against Negative Self-Talk:

- When negative thoughts or feelings of inadequacy arise, remember Romans 8:1: "There is now no condemnation for those who are in Christ Jesus." Condemning self-talk is not from God. Replace negative thoughts with positive affirmations grounded in God's love and acceptance. Remind yourself of your identity as a child of God.

3. Lean on God's Strength:

- Philippians 4:13 tells us that we can do all things through Christ who strengthens us. In moments of weakness or self-doubt, surrender to God's power. Seek His guidance and rely on His strength to face life's challenges with confidence. Pray for His empowerment in every situation.

4. Focus on Pleasing God:

- Galatians 1:10 encourages us to seek the favor of God rather than constantly striving to please others. While it's natural to desire approval from people, remember that your ultimate goal is to honor and please your Heavenly Father. When you prioritize God's approval, you'll find freedom from the burden of seeking validation from others.

5. Affirmations and Declarations:

- Develop a set of positive affirmations and declarations rooted in biblical truths. Use these statements to counteract negative self-talk and build self-confidence. Repeat them daily in moments of doubt. For example, "I am fearfully and wonderfully made" (Psalm 139:14) or "I can do all things through Christ" (Philippians 4:13).

BY IMPLEMENTING these tips into your life, you can move toward a healthier self-image, increased confidence, and a deeper understanding of your unique purpose in God's plan. Remember that your identity is firmly rooted in Christ, and He equips you for every step of your journey.

week seven

DAY 31

Don't Believe Everything You Think

As Bishop Joseph L. Garlington once preached, our words hold tremendous power in shaping our worlds. It's a profound truth I've embraced over the years – what I speak about my life ultimately forges my reality. It's like the scriptures remind us, "Out of the abundance of the heart, the mouth speaks" (Matthew 12:34, ESV).

I made a conscious decision to guard my tongue, for "Death and life are in the power of the tongue" (Proverbs 18:21, ESV). My motto became: "I may think it, but I won't say it." I became quite skilled at this practice. I was so adept at keeping my words kind and positive that one day, during a meeting with my daughter, the speaker talked about speaking with kindness and without judgment. My daughter, known for her quick wit, glanced at me and quipped, "Mom, it's not your words that need to be redeemed; it's your face!" I couldn't help but burst into laughter. But it made me ponder deeply.

My face revealed what my heart concealed. I might not voice my critical thoughts about others or situations, but I certainly entertained them in my mind. Full disclosure: my inner thoughts could be a dark place, and I'm on a daily journey to improve. Why, you ask? Well, as Proverbs 5:21 (TPT) warns,

DAY 31

"For God sees everything you do, and his eyes are wide open as he observes every single habit you have." Yes, every single habit, even those lurking in the shadows of our minds.

I'M NOT HERE to sound legalistic or judgmental. This is a personal struggle I've come to recognize. My thought life sometimes led to unhealthy habits and self-image issues. I extend grace and understanding to others, knowing life's challenges can weigh us down and lead us to make decisions we never intended to make. The struggle is genuine, and I'm no exception. It's ironic that I offer words of encouragement to uplift others, urging them to see themselves through God's eyes, only to harbor self-deprecating thoughts or shoulder blame for the actions of others. It's a twisted paradox, isn't it?

BUT HERE'S the good news – God's grace abounds even in our deepest-seated issues. Trust me; I know this may sound elementary, but it's profoundly transformative. My mother engraved a simple yet powerful scripture in my heart: "I can do all things through Christ who strengthens me" (Philippians 4:13). It adorned the walls of her classroom, adorned sticky notes throughout our home, and echoed in my ears whenever I uttered the dreaded words, "I'll never..." She'd promptly respond, "You can do..." I admit to my teenage eye rolls, but I pause now to repent.

YOU SEE, I know I can change the way I think about myself, my circumstances, and my future. I can renew my mind to be so enveloped by the mind of Christ that I begin to see as He does, hear as He does, and ultimately, think as He does! Will it take time? Undoubtedly. But I take solace in the assurance that "All

DAY 31

things are possible" (Matthew 19:26), and His mercies are new every morning (Lamentations 3:22-23).

Thus, each morning, I pray:

> "Lord, I desire to think as You do, in every aspect and every day. I long to perceive through eyes that transcend this earthly dimension, seeing past my current situation and into the heavenly realm. Your glory surpasses all, and the fleeting struggles of this world are but momentary vapors. I don't merely want to change my perspective; I yearn for Your perspective to become mine, effortlessly. Whatever it takes, I'm willing to do. Whatever You ask of me, I'm ready to give. Wherever You lead, I'm prepared to follow. Reveal Your will to me, and I will take the first step."

In the name of Jesus, amen.

Day 32

Devotion 1: The Power of Our Words

SCRIPTURE:

> PROVERBS 18:21 (ESV) - "DEATH AND LIFE ARE IN THE POWER OF THE TONGUE."

DEAR BROTHERS AND SISTERS,

> ***Reflection***: *Our words have the ability to shape our world, either for the better or for the worse. Just as Bishop Joseph L. Garlington emphasized, what we speak about our lives creates our reality.*
>
> *In your prayer time today, consider the words you have spoken recently. Have they been filled with kindness, encouragement, and life? Or have they contained judgment, negativity, and death? Let us remember the wisdom of the essay's author: "I may think it, but I won't say it." In our thoughts and words, may we strive to reflect the love and grace of our Lord Jesus Christ.*
>
> ***Prayer***: *Heavenly Father, help us guard our*

DAY 32

tongues and use our words to bring life, encouragement, and hope to those around us. May the words of our mouths and the meditations of our hearts be pleasing in Your sight. In Jesus' name, we pray. Amen.

PAUSE AND USE your journal to capture your thoughts

___

___

___

___

___

___

___

___

. . .

DAY 32

Day 33

. . .

Devotion 2: The Battle of the Mind

SCRIPTURE:

> ROMANS 12:2 (NIV) - "DO NOT CONFORM TO THE PATTERN OF THIS WORLD, BUT BE TRANSFORMED BY THE RENEWING OF YOUR MIND."

__Reflection:__ It's essential to recognize that our thoughts can shape our habits, our self-image, and our overall perspective on life. The essay reminds us of the truth found in Romans 12:2: "Do not conform to the pattern of this world, but be transformed by the renewing of your mind."

Take a moment to reflect on your thought life. Are your thoughts aligned with God's perspective, filled with love, grace, and hope? Or do they tend toward negativity and self-criticism? We all face this struggle, but remember that transformation begins with renewing our minds through God's Word and prayer. Let us seek to think as Christ does.

__Prayer:__ Gracious Lord, we surrender our thought

life to You. Help us renew our minds daily through Your Word and the power of Your Spirit. May our thoughts be pleasing to You and bring transformation to our lives. In Jesus' name, we pray. Amen.

SET ASIDE a moment to write down your reflections on what you've read

_____

_____

_____

_____

_____

_____

_____

DAY 33

. . .

Day 34

Devotion 3: The Promise of Renewal

SCRIPTURE:

"LAMENTATIONS 3:22-23 (ESV) - "THE STEADFAST LOVE OF THE LORD NEVER CEASES; HIS MERCIES NEVER COME TO AN END; THEY ARE NEW EVERY MORNING."

Reflection: *We all face struggles within ourselves, including negative self-perception and harmful thought patterns. But take heart, for as Lamentations 3:22-23 reminds us, "The steadfast love of the Lord never ceases; his mercies never come to an end; they are new every morning."*

No matter how deep-seated our issues may be, God's love and grace are greater still. Each day, we have the opportunity to experience His mercy and to transform our thought life. Let us pray with a heart of surrender, as the essay's author did, seeking to think like Jesus and to see the world through His perspective.

Prayer: *Heavenly Father, we thank You for Your steadfast love and unending mercies. Grant us*

DAY 34

the strength to change the way we think, to align our thoughts with Yours, and to experience true renewal. Guide us, Lord, and lead us on this journey of transformation. In Jesus' name, we pray. Amen.

Take a moment to record your thoughts

DAY 34

Day 35

Put What You've Learned into Action

TAKE a pause and embrace a moment of prayerful reflection, immersing yourself in the practical insights at hand. In your journal, map out your unique strategy for weaving these valuable lessons into the fabric of your daily life. By fusing your contemplative spirit with purposeful planning, you'll infuse these principles with the essence of your faith and values, igniting personal growth and deepening your spiritual journey.

GUARD YOUR WORDS AND THOUGHTS:

- As emphasized in this chapter, the words we speak and the thoughts we entertain have a significant impact on our lives. Guard your words by ensuring they are filled with kindness, encouragement, and life. Likewise, be vigilant about your thought life, avoiding negativity, self-criticism, and judgmental thinking.

Daily Renewal of the Mind:

- Make it a daily practice to renew your mind through reading and meditating on God's Word. As Romans 12:2 suggests, transformation comes from the renewing of your mind. Replace negative thought patterns with the truths found in Scripture, and ask the Holy Spirit to guide your thinking.

SEEK ACCOUNTABILITY AND ENCOURAGEMENT:

- Don't face the battle of the mind alone. Seek accountability and encouragement from fellow believers who can support you in your journey to align your thoughts with Christ's perspective. Share your struggles and victories with trusted friends or a mentor.

PRAYER FOR PERSPECTIVE CHANGE:

- Incorporate prayer into your daily routine, just as the essay's author did. Pray for God to help you see the world through His perspective naturally. Surrender your thought life to Him, asking for His guidance, wisdom, and transformation in your thinking.

EMBRACE God's Mercy and Grace:

- Remember that God's love and mercy are renewed every morning, as Lamentations 3:22-23 tells us. When you stumble in your thought life or speech,

DAY 35

do not dwell on guilt or self-condemnation. Instead, embrace God's forgiveness and grace. Start each day with a fresh commitment to align your thoughts and words with His love and truth.

week eight

Day 36

There's Strength in Vulnerability

OVER THE YEARS, I've come to realize that I need to shed the notion of being a superhero and embrace the humility of asking for help. It's perfectly acceptable to seek assistance when we face challenges in our lives. Personally, I've always turned to prayer in times of struggle, finding solace and comfort in the presence of God. My prayer life has been a sanctuary of healing and solace. Yet, the Lord gently reminded me that I also need to be open with my family and close friends, allowing them to be instruments of His guidance in my life.

IN PROVERBS 27:17, it's written, "As iron sharpens iron, so a friend sharpens a friend" (NLT). This biblical wisdom underscores the importance of companionship and the mutual support we can provide to one another. Our friends can play a pivotal role in helping us grow and navigate life's challenges.

DURING A PERIOD OF INTROSPECTION, the Lord impressed upon my heart the need to be H.O.T. – Honest, Open, and Transparent. My desire to be everything to everyone had led me down an unhealthy path of emotional self-destruction. I needed to understand that I am called to be supernatural, not a superhero.

DAY 36

THE LORD DIRECTED my attention to a profound story in the Bible – the account of a man lowered through a roof to reach Jesus by his friends. While I had often marveled at the miraculous healing in this story, the Lord highlighted the remarkable nature of these friends. They recognized that their friend was physically incapable of reaching Jesus on his own, yet they possessed unwavering faith in his healing, even when he might not have had that faith himself.

DESPITE THE CROWDED obstacles in their way, they persevered, refusing to be deterred. They found a way to get their friend to Jesus. Whether or not the lame man had initially asked for help is unknown, but what's clear is that without their assistance, he might have remained lame. Similarly, in our lives, there are moments when we need to be open and vulnerable, seeking help and relying on both our inner strength and the support of covenant friends to guide us through our darkest hours.

JUST AS THOSE friends played a crucial role in bringing healing to the paralyzed man, our friends and loved ones can help us find emotional and spiritual wholeness when we allow them into our struggles. Embracing this biblical wisdom, we learn that seeking assistance and being open about our needs is not a sign of weakness but a testament to our faith in God's plan and His use of earthly companions to sharpen and uplift one another.

Day 37

Devotion 1: Embracing Humility and Seeking Help

SCRIPTURE:

> PROVERBS 3:5-6 (NLT) "TRUST IN THE LORD WITH ALL YOUR HEART; DO NOT DEPEND ON YOUR OWN UNDERSTANDING. SEEK HIS WILL IN ALL YOU DO, AND HE WILL SHOW YOU WHICH PATH TO TAKE."

Reflection: In our journey of faith, we often find ourselves striving to be superheroes, attempting to handle life's challenges on our own. However, as we reflect on Proverbs 3:5-6, we are reminded of the importance of humility. We must trust in the Lord completely and seek His guidance in all aspects of our lives.

It's okay to ask for help, both from God and our trusted friends and family. We are not meant to navigate life's difficulties alone. Let us embrace the humility of seeking assistance when we need it, trusting that God will show us the way. Today, take a moment to reflect on any challenges you're facing and invite God and your loved ones to join you in finding

DAY 37

solutions. Remember, seeking help is a sign of faith and trust in the Lord's plan for your life.

Prayer: *Dear Heavenly Father, In my journey of faith, I sometimes forget that I don't have to be a superhero, handling life's challenges on my own. Proverbs 3:5-6 reminds me to embrace humility and trust in You completely. I understand now that it's okay to ask for help, from both You and my trusted friends and family. I'm not meant to navigate life's difficulties alone. Today, I take a moment to reflect on my challenges and invite You and my loved ones to join me in finding solutions. Seeking help is a sign of my faith and trust in Your plan for my life.*
Amen.

TAKE time to journal your thoughts

. . .

DAY 37

DAY 38

. . .

Devotion 2: Embracing Humility and Seeking Help

SCRIPTURE:

> Proverbs 3:5-6 (NLT)"Trust in the Lord with all your heart; do not depend on your own understanding. Seek his will in all you do, and he will show you which path to take."

REFLECTION: In our journey of faith, we often find ourselves striving to be superheroes, attempting to handle life's challenges on our own. However, as we reflect on Proverbs 3:5-6, we are reminded of the importance of humility. We must trust in the Lord completely and seek His guidance in all aspects of our lives.

It's okay to ask for help, both from God and our trusted friends and family. We are not meant to navigate life's difficulties alone. Let us embrace the humility of seeking assistance when we need it, trusting that God will show us the way. Today, take a moment to reflect on any challenges you're facing and invite God and your loved ones to join you in finding solutions. Remember, seeking help is a sign of faith and trust in the Lord's plan for your life.

. . .

DAY 38

PRAYER: Dear Heavenly Father, In my journey of faith, I sometimes forget that I don't have to be a superhero, handling life's challenges on my own. Proverbs 3:5-6 reminds me to embrace humility and trust in You completely.

I understand now that it's okay to ask for help, from both You and my trusted friends and family. I'm not meant to navigate life's difficulties alone. Today, I take a moment to reflect on my challenges and invite You and my loved ones to join me in finding solutions. Seeking help is a sign of my faith and trust in Your plan for my life.

Amen.

TAKE time to journal your thoughts

_____

_____

_____

_____

_____

_____

. . .

DAY 38

Day 39

Devotion 3: The Power of Covenant Friends

SCRIPTURE:

> ECCLESIASTES 4:9-10 (NLT) "TWO PEOPLE ARE BETTER OFF THAN ONE, FOR THEY CAN HELP EACH OTHER SUCCEED. IF ONE PERSON FALLS, THE OTHER CAN REACH OUT AND HELP. BUT SOMEONE WHO FALLS ALONE IS IN REAL TROUBLE."

Reflection: *Reflecting on the story of the friends who lowered the paralyzed man to Jesus, we are reminded of the power of covenant friends. In Ecclesiastes 4:9-10, we learn that two are better than one because they can support each other in times of need.*

Just as those friends were determined to bring healing to their companion, our covenant friends can be instrumental in our spiritual journey. They are there to lift us up when we fall and to provide support and encouragement when we face challenges. Don't hesitate to reach out to your covenant friends when you need assistance, and be willing to offer your support when they are in need.

DAY 39

Today, take a moment to thank God for the covenant friends He has placed in your life.

Prayer: *Pray for your relationships to be characterized by mutual support and a shared commitment to each other's spiritual growth. Remember that you are not alone in your journey of faith, and together, you can help each other succeed.*

TAKE time to journal your thoughts

_____

_____

_____

_____

_____

_____

_____

. . .

DAY 39

Day 40

. . .

I recommend taking a moment of quiet reflection for prayer, immersing yourself in the practical wisdom offered. In your journal, craft a unique plan for incorporating these valuable insights into your daily life. By combining contemplative thought with strategic planning, you'll bring these principles to life, aligning them with your faith and values to nurture personal growth and deepen your spiritual journey.

Here are five helpful tips based on the themes from the previous chapter:

1. Embrace Humility and Seek God's Guidance:

- Trust in the Lord with all your heart and seek His will in everything you do (Proverbs 3:5-6). Acknowledge that you don't have to be a superhero; it's okay to seek God's wisdom and guidance in your life's decisions and challenges.

2. Practice H.O.T. Communication:

- Be Honest, Open, and Transparent in your relationships (Ephesians 4:25). Authenticity and vulnerability foster deep connections with others. Share your struggles and needs with trusted friends and family, allowing them to support and uplift you.

3. Cultivate Covenant Friendships:

- Build and nurture covenant friendships (Ecclesiastes 4:9-10). Surround yourself with friends who are committed to your well-being and spiritual growth. Offer your support and encouragement to them in return.

4. Be Faithful in Prayer:

- Continue to rely on prayer in times of struggle (Philippians 4:6-7). Prayer is a powerful tool for seeking help and finding comfort in God's presence. Make prayer a regular part of your life, bringing both your joys and burdens to the Lord.

5. Extend Help to Others:

- Be the kind of friend who helps lower others to Jesus (Mark 2:1-5). Just as the friends of the paralyzed man went to great lengths to assist their friend, look for opportunities to support and uplift those in need. Sometimes, you may be the answer to someone else's prayers.

INCORPORATING these tips into your life can help you grow spiritually, build meaningful relationships, and navigate life's challenges with the support of both God and trusted friends.

. . .

DAY 40

As we draw this book to a close, my hope is that our journey together through the realms of soul detoxing has left you with a newfound understanding of the significance of nurturing your inner self. Though we've only scratched the surface of this topic we've discovered the essential concept of tending to our souls for emotional and spiritual wholeness.

In this exploration, we've discovered that soul detoxing isn't confined to religious beliefs or dogma; it's a universal concept that transcends doctrine and speaks to our shared human experience. It's about acknowledging that, much like we make choices to nourish our bodies with wholesome foods, we can make choices to cultivate our inner selves with positive thoughts, emotional healing, and spiritual growth.

The parallels between our bodily health and the state of our souls are undeniable. Just as we examine food labels to make informed dietary choices, we can examine the contents of our hearts and minds to make choices that uplift and cleanse our souls. It's about becoming conscious of the emotional baggage we carry and taking the steps to release it.

We've seen how the wisdom of Scriptures and practical steps converge in this journey. Whether it's the cleansing of our hearts as spoken of in Psalm 51, or the importance of guarding our inner selves as emphasized in Proverbs 4:23, there's a resonance in the message that transcends religious boundaries. It's a call to recognize the sanctity of our inner selves and to take responsibility for their well-being.

. . .

DAY 40

JUST AS WE'VE learned to honor our bodies as temples of the Holy Spirit, we must care for our souls so that we can be vessels the Lord can work through effectively. By doing so, we can embrace the virtues of love, joy, peace, kindness, and self-control as outlined in Galatians 5:22-23. These virtues emanate from a purified soul, guiding us towards a life that aligns with our deepest values and desires.

IN CLOSING, I encourage you to continue on this path of soul detoxing, for it's not a one-time endeavor but a lifelong journey. Much like maintaining physical health requires consistent effort, nurturing our souls demands ongoing attention and care. As we part ways, remember that taking care of your soul is a precious form of self-love, and you are worthy of this journey.

MAY your soul be a sanctuary of peace, love, and serenity, where emotional baggage is released, and spiritual growth flourishes. And, in the words of our earlier discussion, may you find the harmony and balance that your triune self – spirit, soul, and body – truly deserve. With gratitude for sharing this transformative journey, I bid you farewell for now, knowing that our paths may cross again in the beautiful tapestry of life. Until then, may you walk in the light of self-awareness, inner peace, and soulful rejuvenation. God bless you.

bibliography

The Holy Bible: English Standard Version. (2016). (Jn 15:5–8). Wheaton, IL: Crossway Bibles.

The Holy Bible: English Standard Version. (2016). (Jn 15:5–8). Wheaton, IL: Crossway Bibles.

The New International Version. (2011). (Mk 11:12–14). Grand Rapids, MI: Zondervan.

The Holy Bible: English Standard Version. (2016). (2 Co 4:8–9). Wheaton, IL: Crossway Bibles.

Tyndale House Publishers. (2015). *Holy Bible: New Living Translation* (So 2:15). Carol Stream, IL: Tyndale House Publishers.

Tyndale House Publishers. (2015). Holy Bible: New Living Translation (2 Co 5:17). Carol Stream, IL: Tyndale House Publishers.

The Holy Bible: English Standard Version. (2016). (2 Co 3:18). Wheaton, IL: Crossway Bibles.

The Holy Bible: English Standard Version. (2016). (Ro 8:14–16). Wheaton, IL: Crossway Bibles.

Tyndale House Publishers. (2015). Holy Bible: New Living Translation (Ga 3:26–29). Carol Stream, IL: Tyndale House Publishers.

Tyndale House Publishers. (2015). *Holy Bible: New Living Translation* (La 3:22–24). Carol Stream, IL: Tyndale House Publishers

Tyndale House Publishers. (2015). *Holy Bible: New Living Translation* (Mt 6:31–33). Carol Stream, IL: Tyndale House Publishers.

ways to connect with the author

Website:
www.billandlynne.com

Ministry:
Restoring the Soul Retreat Reset Classes
Oasis City Church
Covenant Church of Pittsburgh
Women's Emerge Conference

Socials:
Facebook: Lynne Themelaras
X: Lynne Themelaras
Instagram: Lynne Themelaras / Bill & Lynne Themelaras